Satan, Be Gone:
ISSA Movement

KK

Thanks for
you support!

04 / 13 / 18

The Lord has great
things in store for you!

Satan, Be Gone:
ISSA Movement

Kristerfur Reed

"I just wanna say thank you so much, not only to God, but to Jesus. Because, ya know, I wouldn't be here without him. He has really blessed me. He's put me in this position, so I wanna say thank you so much…"

—Justin Bieber

Acknowledgments

Before all else, I want to thank my mother, Minister Dorothy Borders. I love you.

I also want to thank my aunt, Pastor Arfaye Paylor, for her continued support. In addition to her, thanks to my Godmother, Pastor Lolita Luckett, and all my family and friends.

Thank you to my publisher, Taneisha Naylor (author of *Pregnant with a Purpose* and *Born With A Purpose*), and her company, Lifted Publishing, for working with me and answering all my questions.

Thank you to fellow author, TiTanya Johnson "Lady Ty" (Author of *Daddy Issues*), for being a friend, helping me build a closer relationship with God, and helping me find a church.

Thank you to Coach Sophia Ruffin "The Comeback Kid" (Author of *From Point Guard to Prophet*) for believing in me, coaching me, and pouring into me. Also, thank you to the entire Comeback Kid Squad. I love you guys.

Thank you to Deidre, Genese, and Stephanie Daniels, my new family, for sowing into me, believing in me, and letting God use you. I love you!

Thank you to Apostle Beverly London and God Cares For You International Ministries for speaking into my life when no one else would.

Most importantly, thank you to YOU, the readers. It is my earnest prayer that this book and my story bless you. I pray this project sends you hope that better days are coming, no matter what you may face. I pray the Holy Spirit allows you to walk in total deliverance. I pray you are encouraged.

Disclaimer

I am a twenty-year-old millennial. I have absolutely no "formal" ministerial training. If you are looking for a deep author with twelve honorary doctorates, you have purchased the wrong memoir. All thoughts and opinions on scripture in this book are strictly things I have deduced from life experiences, prior to writing. All teachings on deliverance have been divinely inspired (given to me by the Holy Ghost or the spirit of prophecy). I wrote this book for real people with real problems who are in need of deliverance. It is not for pretentious "church folk." If that is you, get ready to be offended.

Contents

Introduction

Issa Movement

An important thing I learned about deliverance while writing this and living my own life is that deliverance is a lifestyle. It is so much more than coughing up phlegm and crying in church. Deliverance is the continual process of waking up every morning, remembering how good you felt when you were sinning, and deciding that living for God is far more desirable. Speaking as a former (fill in the blank), that is a very hard thing to do.

God spoke to me and said that, before anything else, *Satan, Be Gone* is not a book; it is a movement. A book can only be bought and read, but a movement can and will be lived. People struggling with the process of leaving sin need to have a strong sense of community in their lives to ground them in their new values. Those across the world who buy this book are uniting together in spirit, and as God grows this movement, we will even meet in real life.

The phrase "Satan, Be Gone" holds a large amount of spiritual weight. I came up with it while reading about Jesus and Peter in Matthew 16. Peter had, for lack of better words, been cutting up, and Jesus was entirely fed up with it. He said in verse 23, "Get behind me, Satan! You are a stumbling block to me; you do not have in mind the concerns of God, but merely human concerns." I love this passage of scripture so much, and even though this really pertains to the devil being in your associates rather than in your own life, we still need to tell the devil to get out of our space (mentally and physically). My generation probably would have said, "HOP OFF!", but that one isn't for church folk.

My desire is that this project will encourage my generation to stand up, kick the devil out of their lives, and live holy before God. I believe that if we come together in this new age holiness movement, the world would be changed for the better. This is not like Pentecostal holiness movements of the past. We're not trying to put doilies and lap scarves on women or dress men like members of the Ku Klux Klan. My heart's desire is that an *internal* holiness would arise in God's people so that the world cannot help but see it on our outsides.

Part 1

The Story:
An Unadulterated Testimony

Chapter One

Early Onset Rejection

"They triumphed over him by the blood of the Lamb and by the word of their testimony…"
[Revelation 12:11]

If you just bought this book or are in your local bookstore considering the purchase, I'm sure you're in need of deliverance from something or have received some type of deliverance in the past. What is deliverance, you ask? According to Merriam-Webster, it means "liberation or the state of being rescued."

We all need to be liberated or rescued from something, but everyone's circumstances are different. That is why there are different types of deliverance. One form of deliverance is geographical deliverance. This is where you are in the wrong place and must be transported to the right place. We often see geographical deliverances occur in film. You know how it goes: there's a damsel in distress and the hero arrives just in time to rescue her. A biblical form of the scenario is when Moses led the children of Israel out of captivity.

My point is that, even though scenarios differ, deliverance is a necessity across a variety of platforms. Pay attention because this is a nugget of wisdom: the secret to receiving real deliverance is...there is no secret! A lot of people walk out of a sin, start fasting and praying for the renewal of their mind, yet do not believe they are "really delivered" because they continue to have thoughts reminiscent of their old lives. An uneducated person would allow these thoughts to make them believe they are not fully delivered, but since you and I are biblical scholars we know the Bible says in John 8:36: "Whom the SON sets free is free indeed."

When you are liberated, nothing can bind you again unless you allow yourself to be bound. Let that be your mindset. This book is about my deliverance and how you can be delivered by renouncing your old ways, dealing with your hurts, and telling your story. I've completed the first step. I am still working on the second every day, and if you read on, you'll see me do the third. Now, let's get delivered together.

Do me a favor and picture a fall evening in late 2001. Four-year-old me was in my parents' bed, watching "Big Momma's House" on VHS. If you have seen that film, you know there is a scene where actress Nia Long gets in bed with her grandmother (Martin Lawrence in drag) because she is afraid of the lightning storm taking place in the movie.

While I was watching the movie, Chicago happened to also be experiencing a thunderstorm. My parents were in the living room arguing as per usual, and I turned up the volume to drown their voices. I also decided to hit the light switch while I was up to view the television better.

The movie played, and in perfect sync, a flash of lightning thrust out in the film and another against my actual window pane. I jumped off the bed, and as soon as my feet hit the floor, the fattest roach I have ever seen shot out from underneath the bed, went over my feet, and ran in circles in front of the television stand.

I flailed and screamed for someone to kill it. My father marched in the room to find his firstborn and only son crying over an insect. And he, attempting to build character in me, picked up the roach and threw it on me. I don't remember my exact reaction as I've spent many years trying to blot out this memory, but as you can probably assume, it was far from the surge of masculinity the average dad would've been hoping for.

If you can take a moment and wipe your eyes from the second-hand embarrassment I just gave you, think about how you would have acted in my shoes. Roaches, in my extremely educated vernacular, are freaking gross. Who wants one thrown on them? But if I had known that my "feminine" reaction was going to displease my father, I would have attempted to put on

9

a front. This was my earliest encounter with a spirit that I'd later become best friends with: rejection.

My dad, whom I am partially named after, is seventeen years older than my fifty-two-year-old mother and was born and raised in Natchez, Mississippi. If you know anything about Mississippi during the 1940s, you know that black men were trained to carry themselves a certain way: machismo. My dad wore a certain cologne, the smell of which remained in the room after he left. He played the saxophone. He was a womanizer. My dad was cool—a black James Bond. And possibly while viewing me rip my clothes off and take flight because of an insect, he realized his successor did not possess ANY of those same qualities. I felt like a disappointment in that moment. I took those lesser feelings, which he didn't intentionally displace on me, into every other part of my life after that night.

Home was not always happy for me, in the earlier years at least. Someone in that apartment (between my father, mother, and me) was always disappointed in someone. My parents ended up having what I like to affectionately call a "common law divorce." And in true fashion of the rolling stone he was, I didn't see my dad for a few years after my parents separated. My mother and I moved in with my grandmother and my uncle in the small town of Calumet Park, Illinois, USA. The population is 7,787. And to answer your next question, "Yes, everyone does know everyone."

I went to grade school in the neighboring town, Blue Island. It was a Catholic institution, predominately white and Latino. My class, from preschool to the

11

eighth grade, had the same twelve kids in it.
I liked school, but I got in trouble for
talking too much. Often. My dad began to
make sporadic visits around the time I hit
second grade. He would show up and ask if I
was "playing football yet." I would shoot
him a look that subtly said, "HELL NO," and
he would be on his way. My dad openly
disapproved of me. I felt like he, and all
men, thought I wasn't good enough. I
didn't play any sports, and I was afraid of
bugs. In grade school logic, I basically
wasn't a man, and he made attempts to
toughen me up.

One summer, my father decided it was
time I learned how to ride a bike. He came
over, and I was ecstatic to see him. We were
finally going to have a father/son moment.
I got on the bike and rode a little bit, under
his instruction, until I fell off and skinned

my knee. I started crying, and he called me a punk. Needless to say, I never learned how to ride a bike.

My dad and I being at odds caused my mom and me to be super tight. She was my best friend. I was always with her, and I would be irate when I was not. I honestly struggled interacting with children my own age. This may have been because I was an only child and grew up in a house with a senior citizen and her two middle-aged kids (my mother and uncle). My occasional babysitter was my cousin, and she was older than my mom. So that was another person in their golden years for me to converse with.

As I progressed in school, I eventually became better at speaking with the other kids. I even made some friends, but I knew I was different from all of them. For starters, I loved talking about Jesus. I don't know if this was because my mom liked church and I wanted to be like her or if God was ministering to me at a young age. But discussing religion was not a common ground with other eight-year-olds. This caused me to exclusively have friends at church, namely girls.

When I was about nine, my mother became a minister, which meant that I became what the Christian community called a "PK" (a preacher's kid). We started regularly attending a Baptist church by our house. I remember not particularly caring for it at first until I met the youth pastor and became acquainted with the children's church department. I went for months and grew a fire for the things of God. I asked my mom if I could get baptized and eventually did. It was lit, and I wanted to share this feeling I had with all my friends.

One evening after Sunday service, the ministers (and their children) gathered for a party. I was the type of kid who loved talking to adults and people older than I. My mom always hated that I talked to her friends. She said her friends were for HER, and mine were for me.

I was the only boy my age at this church party. The couple who threw it had a son a year or so younger than I, but we didn't speak. I tried to hang out with my mom, but she made me leave. Since I was very close to my mother, her brushing me off hurt my feelings, but from what I hear, everything happens for a reason. Rejection had crept in again, and this wasn't even the bad part.

I hung out with the other boy. I tried to make casual conversation, but it wasn't bubbly and light. I had issues talking with other kids and ran out of things to talk about. My dad not being around made it difficult for me to interact with other males, as well, so this situation was not ideal. We joked with each other, but I felt awkward after a while. I wasn't like other little boys. Before I knew what had happened, he pulled down my pants and started massaging my legs.

In the early 1920s, Professor Walter Bradford Cannon coined a theory named the "Fight or Flight Response." This suggests that when mammals are faced with immediate danger, we naturally decide within the first three to five seconds to defend ourselves or flee. On this evening, Professor Cannon's theory was proven wrong. Seconds, minutes, and what felt like hours had passed, yet I was frozen in time. My mind drew a blank. I didn't know if I was supposed to like the touching or not. I did not know if...I did not know anything at that moment.

I don't remember what happened after my pants came off. He didn't touch my genitals but asked to see them; I remember that much. I ran out of the room to tell my mother something bad had happened. I tried to whisper in her ear that I had been touched by someone, but I didn't exactly know how to say it. I finally mustered up the courage to softly say, "S-s-someone t-t-t-touched me," under an orchestra of whimpers. My mother turned her head and sharply told me to "stop lying" and to sit my "little tail down." I could do nothing but sit at the bottom of her chair and cry. Her friends (all other ordained ministers) felt uncomfortable—as they should have—trying to enjoy themselves with a crying eight-year-old boy in the room. Everyone was silent until my mom and I left.

My mom was angry at me for embarrassing her at the party. She thought I was lying for attention when I said I got—whatever it was that had taken place in that room. On the ride home, anxiety brewed within me. Contemplating my mother bringing up what happened, I didn't know if I could muster up the courage to even say it a second time. I sat silently in the passenger seat. That was, to this day, the longest car ride of my life. Vomit roiled in my stomach. I was sickened with premonitions that my mother would yell at me for the rest of my life for embarrassing her. The thought of being fondled, publicly embarrassed, called a liar, and eternally berated was entirely too taxing.

I wept as we drove home, while my mother yelled in the background. She looked at me when we turned onto our block and said, "Why are you still crying? What is wrong with you?" I could do nothing but faintly say, "I already told you." We pulled into the driveway. I hurried into the house and woke my grandmother to tell her what happened. She called my mother into the room and asked me to leave.

Do you remember how important being right was when you were a kid? At my school we would tease each other with phrases, such as "I told you so…neener neener neener." I'm sure you're familiar with them. Imagine being a child who had been sexually "enlightened" with an unwelcome advance and not being believed. I was infuriated and in pain. I was right, but no one believed me. When my mother realized I wasn't lying, she came to me and apologized. As you can imagine, I was not eager about accepting. I didn't know what went on between her and my grandmother, but I knew I would still have to go to school the next day.

Ironically, in class the following day, we began a program named Child Lures. We were taught that if we were ever touched by anyone (by other kids or an adult), we could tell a parent, teacher, or religious leader and receive help. Pardon my French, but I could do nothing but sit and think this was complete crap. I had just experienced inappropriate touching, and NO ONE BELIEVED ME until I was miles away from the person who did it. I told myself, at eight years old, that other people could not be trusted. I hated school after that moment. It was all pointless to me.

I did trust an older cousin. She, a member of the LGBT community, was my babysitter whenever my mom had to run an errand or preach. My cousin and I grew extremely close. I would go to her girlfriends' homes with her all the time, not even knowing they were her partners. She never kissed a woman in front of me, but she had a beard and wore a durag. Her mother, a Missionary Baptist Sunday school teacher, was unamused. I saw them argue and berate each other countless times. I knew if I ever had "special feelings" as my cousin did that I could not speak of it because all heck would break loose in my family—a family that often confused me. In one breath, they confessed the love of Christ, and in the next, they were at each other's throats. And the entire time, around all of these so-called spirit-filled believers, I was having sexual identity crises before the age of ten and no one knew. I was my mother's only child, and yet I was a child slipping through the cracks. The only person I wanted to speak to was my older cousin, but since everyone felt something was wrong with her, I was afraid to say anything to her.

Before we continue, I'd be remiss if I didn't say there were great moments in my childhood, as well. For instance, I wrote a short story in the third grade that my teacher thought was so good she paid for it to get published. I had a lot of cool things happen to me, but the funny thing about having a spirit of rejection is that you tend to only focus on the negative situations. This is because that spirit places you in the mindset that your negatives outweigh your positives. Rejection, as defined by Merriam-Webster, is "the state of being rejected." Reject means to "cast off, throwback, repulse." It is also listed as "refusal of acceptance, consideration, or submission." You get the point: it means something is unwanted.

I felt my father rejected me for not being masculine enough, and the fact we couldn't even figure out my bicycle without arguing did not help the situation. I had deduced that because I was "soft" I could never be friends with or work with men unless, of course, it was sexual. The boy who rubbed me seemed to enjoy me, and I felt welcomed in that situation. Maybe God wanted me to be sexual with men. Do you see where my mind was?

Rejection also led me to feel that I was without a voice. I cried out to my mother, and she did not believe me. Her first presumption was that I was telling her some sort of fable. What kind of person would assume that a kid is lying about sexual things? The enemy had so many open doors in my life.

I became angry while typing this first chapter because I realized the enemy had striped me of my only resource. As I said earlier, I loved church as a kid. I didn't know too much about God, but I loved hearing the uplifting music and the youth leader teach. But after being touched by a member of the church, I no longer wanted to go. I felt as if God had let me down. God made me sick, and I cursed him. Rejection can put you in crazy mental places.

Chapter 2

Eye for an Eye

"An eye for an eye leaves the whole world blind."
—Anonymous

Middle school was an interesting time of my life. As I said, I didn't really talk to other guys, so everyone in the school called me gay. I remember hating school so much and returning home, crying to my mother. She would always tell me to pray. I thought to myself, What the heck is that going to do?

My mom's response to everything was to tell me to pray about it. In a way, it made me feel as if she either didn't know how to help me solve my problems or just didn't care. Why was I being told to pray when I was crying out for advice?

Parents often say things like that regularly, though. "Go play outside. Adults are in here talking." Whenever I see this happen, I always want to ask the parent, "Have you ever thought that Jimmy came to you because he wanted something important?" How negligent.

The bullying grew worse and worse. I dealt with it by watching porn in my spare time. I had seen my first one from a classmate. I don't remember if it was at a sleepover or in school, but I was introduced to it nonetheless. It was self-soothing. I felt disgusted after watching these movies, but I also couldn't stop. It was like an addiction or stronghold had set up in that area, yet every man I spoke to about it told me the behavior was normal. I stopped worrying about it eventually even though I knew something was wrong.

How did I know it was wrong? For starters, I had to find the videos in the "private browser" and wait until everyone around me was asleep. Moral things don't generally require secrecy. I spoke to Christian friends, but they shared that they did it, too, so I continued. "God knew my heart." That's the excuse we're supposed to use, right?

My school had spring musicals and fall plays. I would usually be cast in an important role, and I remember thinking that was cool. I wasn't a sporty kid, so being considered talented was a big deal. Everyone in my class played basketball or volleyball. I was unique for acting, and I liked that.

"Feeling myself" from being the star of the school plays, I became a bully. Kids in my class had lisps or other noticeable flaws, and I'd poke fun at them all day. This was another form of self-soothing for me. I felt good about myself making jokes and having everyone laugh and be entertained at someone else's expense for a change. Did you know that most bullies have been bullied before? It's almost like a sick survival of the fittest. Kill or be killed.

Believe it or not, I was not only a bully to students. The teachers were victims of my bullying, as well, especially the eighth grade teacher. She was meek and easy to manipulate. Most would think controlling a class of twelve is an easy task, but my teacher failed multiple times. Some days, I would walk in and argue with other students, and our fighting would last all day. The teacher just sat and completed crossword puzzles.

I really regret that time of my life. I was mean to other people, but I am a living witness that you reap what you sow. At the end of middle school, all the "friends" I had made who always laughed at my jokes deserted me. I was alone. In a last attempt to get a laugh, I pulled the fire alarm a few days before graduation. My mom was really upset with me, and I got expelled.

I moved on to high school, which opened a lot of doors for me, good and bad. I competed on the debate team, which I loved. My first three years of school were not the best, but senior year was great. I had made a lot of friends by that point, and I was more comfortable with myself (or who I was at the time, at least).

New Year's Eve of my senior year was the first time I had sex with another guy. I thought I was finally embracing my true self in that moment. Since everybody had told me this was who I was my entire life, I might as well agree, right? I remember the experience being liberating and the perfect middle finger to my Christian family that I had begun to despise.

I graduated high school and had sex with a lot more men. I remember coming out of the closet to my mother and her telling me she knew the entire time, but she also told me that being gay was not what God had intended for my life. I wanted to ask, "As an ordained minister, if you've known that I've had a 'demon' my whole life, why would you not perform an exorcism? C'mon, make me throw up, rotate my head, and make me vomit pea soup like the girl in the exorcist." It was a complete joke. I did not respect my mother at all at that moment. Mind you, no one was saying it was a "demon" but me. Amazing! Luke 6:45 says that "...the mouth speaks what the heart is full of." I didn't know if this was really wrong or not, but it felt good. I kept going.

"Mind you, no one was saying it was a "demon" but me."

This led to my coming out of the closet to others, day by day. I truly embraced being gay or queer or whatever other obscure word homosexuals identify with now. I graduated high school and attended gay pride events where I was fascinated to meet drag queens. I had never realized that men wore women's clothing and were comfortable doing so. I saw men wearing heels and lipstick and wigs with no one commenting on it or even batting an eyelash—a false one, of course.

I can't necessarily say that was something I was comfortable with at the time. But they looked free and happy, and in the state of depression I was secretly in, I was willing to mock anything even remotely close to happiness. I was a modern hippie, in my opinion. I'd go to the parade, drink liquor off the cooler from a street vendor, have sex with a guy, and catch the train home in the morning. This was the life.

I've realized that this time of my life occurred because of what I like to call spirit roots. A spirit root is the base reason why you partake in ungodly behavior. It is normally planted in your life as a child and flourishes when you mishandle negative situations. I was bullied for not acting like other kids, so I retaliated by becoming a bully and hurting others.

> "*A spirit root is the base reason why you partake in ungodly behavior.*"

Retaliation is the spirit root (we as Christians know the Bible says that only God has the right to repay, for all vengeance is His). I was called gay my entire life. This made me lash out and hate homosexual people for a long time (before I ended up in the lifestyle, of course). What do you think the spirit root is in that scenario? It can't be name-calling, because that was done to me and not something I did to another.

The spirit root in this situation is retaliation, again. If revenge belongs to God, then what right do we have as people to hate others for wronging us? Are hatred and anger not forms of retaliation? Let us walk in forgiveness and release all our stress unto the only one who can deal with our burdens: God.

Chapter 3

Jumping off the Ledge

"For the mind that is set on the flesh is hostile to God, for it does not submit to God's law; indeed, it cannot."
[Romans 8:7 ESV]

I entered college, and it wasn't going as I had hoped. I decided to deal with it the only way I knew how: sex. This caused me to start frequenting "Boystown," the gay area in Chicago, more often, where I walked around and refreshed gay apps. There are apps that tell you the exact location of the closest gay; including his name, a brief "description," and most likely a nude photograph. You can meet up, drop trou, and be about your way. And when I found out that certain homosexual men fetishized young black men, I was on cloud nine.

For lack of better words, I entered the world of sex work. Men would message me asking for nude photos, videos, or even to meet up and do certain acts. I would go, do what I had to do, and collect money. It was a thrill for me at the time. I grew up in a family that often fought over money. I remember being younger and listening to my grandmother and mother verbally joust over rent. Being broke at this particular time—most college students are, from what I hear, at least—you can say I thought my decision would be lucrative and eventful.

I made friends who were also doing this type of work, and they told me about websites where I could go on camera and be sent money in exchange for performing acts that people requested. I was involved in this for a long period of time. It was so easy, and I loved the fast money.

At school, I registered at the last minute for classes, so I was unable to pick and choose my professors and ended up with some real nuts. One of my math professors was known for being stern. One of the foreign students was repeatedly berated by this professor. She would patronize us so much that I would skip class.

The thing about people who deal with or have dealt with the spirit of rejection before is that we tend to lack integrity. I believe people do not speak out about injustices because rejection has made them feel their voices no longer matter. It was easier to avoid class than to address the issue, so that is what I did. Granted, speaking with the professor or the student board about how I felt we were treated may have not amounted to anything, but I would have been courageous and integral for taking a stand. I brought up rejection again because it tends to spill into every aspect of our lives and has lingering effects.

I watched a lot of television shows with drag queens in this era of my life. I was interested in going to a drag show, but I was only nineteen. I forget how I came about seeing a particular flyer, but I saw a gay bar by my home was having a drag competition. I told everyone at my on-campus job that I would be competing so they would support me. I even reunited with old friends from grammar school, who I knew would help me get ready. I remember being so infatuated with cross-dressing that I stopped showing up for classes, sometimes school all together, or I showed up for work study and left. I knew I was going to become famous. I spent months watching YouTube videos and talking to friends in beauty school, trying to piece together a persona.

I grabbed close friends of mine and went to different places to buy makeup. Then, whenever I had an opportunity to be home alone, I would do my face, take pictures, and post them online in underground drag community forums. Other queens would give me advice on makeup and other key items to buy.

One day, I accidentally sent a picture to someone I went to church with, and they screenshotted it and showed it to others. My feelings were hurt by this, and I felt as if I could not return to the church. Everyone would ridicule me.

This is another side effect of rejection: conceit. You think, because you spend the day swishing your flaws around in your head, that everyone is mulling over your flaws, as well. I proceeded to swim farther away from God and more into that lifestyle.

One day, after being dismissed early from work, I decided to go to the beauty supply to look at wigs. It was payday, so this was the perfect time. This was around 11:00 a.m. on an early September day in Palos Heights, Illinois. The weather was beautiful and warm. No one was on the road. I sat in the school parking lot looking for music to play. My pulling out of the parking lot "scene" had to be set just right.

Before I pulled out, I opened my self-sealed envelope check, signed the back, and put it on the passenger seat. I drove and realized I was going the wrong way. I checked my mirrors and began to make a U-turn. In the middle of my turn, a car I apparently had missed beforehand was charging at me. I had no choice but to skip the curb, attempting to avoid a collision. I drove over the curb and tried to decelerate, only to discover my brakes had finally given out. If you have ever been to college and financed your own education, you know the struggle of a brake light being on for months. I couldn't stay on top of paying for classes, bills, gas, and keeping the car in "tip top" shape on $8.25 an hour. I had made the poor choice of letting the brakes become a lesser priority, and life was about to teach me a lesson.

Maneuvering my car onto the curb, I slammed on the brakes, not realizing they'd gone kaput. My car slid between three poles and violently slammed into an electrical servicing pole. The door caved in and the mirrors were shaved off. Trapped in the car, I had an outer body experience.

I reached for my phone to call 9-1-1. They would be able to pry me out of the car as I'd seen in every action film. When I faintly smelled gasoline, I started crying because I knew exactly what was about to happen. My car crackled, grumbled, and sizzled as I frantically tried to collect the drag in my backseat. A month's worth of time had gone into secretly hiding these items in my car, and if my car was going to blow up, my things and I were not going down with it. I put everything in my knapsack and tried to pry open the door. It was no use. Smoke rose, and I realized it was finally happening. Those church people were right. I had not gotten my life "right" and was about to go to Hell. In flames I'd burn up, and in even hotter fire I'd spend an eternity. I repented, but I honestly figured there was no point. What kind of

God would have me be ridiculed in school, sexually perverted by Christians (His supposed children), and made me a homosexual only to tell me it was wrong. I didn't believe in God anymore, but I knew if He was real, Hell was where I'd dwell. The engine continued to roar.

While I wallowed in self-pity and contemplated my ultimate demise, a Caucasian woman opened my door. She unclasped my seatbelt and carried me across the street. I remember looking back, seeing the door busted and the knob broken off. I have no clue how she got the door open, outside of a miracle. The car sparked while smoke and small flames peeped out from the engine. The lady who helped get me to safety had to leave, but she called 9-1-1 before her exit.

I sat across the street, not knowing whether to thank God or catch my breath, when it hit me. I had left my money on the seat in the flaming car. As I said earlier, I come from a poor family. Money meant a lot to us, and I wasn't about to let mine slip away. I ran across the street to my flaming vehicle and grabbed my check before the police showed up.

I remember the look on my mother's and grandmother's faces when they saw the car and found I was alive. They were so grateful, but honestly I was just confused. I believe God was trying to get my attention that day. He wanted to stop me before I was too far gone. But like every other problem in my life, I ignored it.

There is a phrase in the church that comes to mind: "There's always warning before destruction." This isn't scriptural, but it is very true. I had no respect for myself. I'm sad to think how my family must have viewed me during this time of my life, but I'm more saddened to think how God viewed me. I know He still loved me, and at times I didn't know what to think about that. Imagine someone you love being regularly stupid and all you can do is watch him destroy himself. I did that daily.

Chapter 4

Community

"For if we go on sinning deliberately after receiving the knowledge of the truth, there no longer remains a sacrifice for sins."
[Hebrews 10:26]

A few months later, the night of the competition neared. My friends and I pulled up to the bar. Because we were late, I had to immediately jump on stage and perform. I was a college dropout and an amateur pornstar.

Growing up in church, it had been prophesied to me, countless times by countless leaders, that I would minister and prophesy internationally, and be wealthy. But the manifestation of this word had taken so long that I thought it would never come. As a result, I gave up on God's plan for my life and let the devil have his way. I got on stage, competed, and took second place.

I sought help after this. Drag was fun and an opportunity to explore a world where I knew God would not be, or so I thought. As I've previously stated, I'd begun to hate church. And because I thought that God was church, this idealism made me despise Him, as well. As I type this and reflect on that night, I am filled with tears. I remember this being one of the happiest days of my life and was blissfully unaware I had sold my soul to the devil (and this wasn't even the first time).

In the gay community, transgender people and drag performers have faux-parents. Since homosexuality has been repetitively controversial through generations, gay people (some of whom have been put out of their homes as teens for "coming out of the closet") band together and enter a covenant with each other. This is likened to how religious leaders have spiritual mentors or medical workers intern before fully released into their respective positions. In these gay families, you have a gay mother (or in my case, a Drag Mom), a gay father, and the list goes on. In joining these families you have to change your name and take non-verbal oaths. This made me uncomfortable, but I knew I wasn't the best performer and that if I joined a gay family I'd learn how to sew, make hair, and do other things that would benefit me in this life. In a sense, I left home and began to do this once I joined a family. I had entered covenant with my new relatives.

There are gay films and documentaries, such as "Paris is Burning" or "Stonewall," that go farther in depth about this family aspect. I can only offer my point of view. Personally, I see this as an outward manifestation of the spirit of rejection.

Yes, I'm talking about that again. It comes up a lot, I know. A group of people who have spent their lives being rejected, for being themselves, come together and form a clique. This gives them the power to accept or reject others who want to be a part of their group. The rejects become the rejecters. Sounds a lot like church, huh?

My gay mother and I spent a lot of time together. I considered him to be a best friend. We spoke about our pasts and discovered we were both victims of molestation as children. He said that his experience with molestation was the reason he became homosexual. I, on the other hand, thought I was gay my whole life because I was different and presumed that was why I had been molested. I also assumed the person who touched me thought I would like it.

Nevertheless, when I began to hang around my gay mother more he revealed a secret to me. He was not actually gay—or so he said. He was dating a woman who I later got to meet over the course of some months. He only did drag because it was lucrative. He was an excellent performer.

Apparently, he had been a minister of music and a mime minister prior to his drag career, which was a recurring theme amongst the black drag queens. His girlfriend and I spoke more and discovered we were both preachers' kids. We bonded over that. I became close with her. I was becoming family.

My gay mother and I began to tour. Do not be fooled; these were no Super Bowl halftime show sized performances by any means. But I was having fun going to different states, including clubs in Chicago. I began to liberally drink. I would get drunk, get in drag, perform, smoke, and get drunk again. I was living it up and living it big. My gay mother did not have his license, so I would drive his car when we had to go places. I loved this because my car had been destroyed, and it was liberating to be back on the road, even driving drunk.

One particular night, my drag mom's girlfriend (confusing, isn't it?) needed to visit a cousin. We pulled up to her relative's apartment complex and dropped her off, and when I got ready to leave the parking lot, my "mom" said to drive to the back. I was confused, but I wasn't going to argue with family. This is a good time to tell you that I was nineteen years old and my gay mother (who I've named Rick for the duration of this book) was around twenty-six. As I told you earlier, I was always around older people. My gay family had to sneak me into clubs and constantly teased me about my age. After reading this, I'm sure you're as surprised as I am that Rick told me a fifteen-year-old guest would be joining us in the car. What was he doing with a fifteen-year-old? Was he a cousin? Was he a nephew or a family friend? Rick opened up a gay dating app called Jack'd. (This was similar to the apps I mentioned previously, but it was primarily used by gay men of color.) He messaged our guest and the young guy came downstairs.

I knew what was about to happen and was very uncomfortable, but when you go to the devil's territory, you are subject to everything affiliated with it. Rick told me to stay seated, and he got out of the car. He embraced the young boy, and they passionately kissed. This sickened me. Rick had told me stories of how he was molested at a young age and listened to my experiences. And now, he was about to commit statutory rape (or so I thought). I wanted to cry. Do I call the police? Do I tell anyone? If the boy's parents found out and discovered that I knew, would I also go to jail? And then, the real question hit me. Was I obligated to tell Rick's girlfriend that he was sleeping with and dating men behind her back?

> *"…when you go to the devil's territory, you are subject to everything affiliated with it."*

I had spent most of my life keeping secrets, and being gay was supposed to be my freedom. I was going to be colorful, loud, and sexually liberated. I never realized I would be watching older men date kids. I realized then that this lifestyle carried aspects of sexual perversion. It is arguable that someone of any sexual orientation can carry the traits of pedophilia. That argument is truthful and valid, but I am here to discuss the one I am familiar with: being gay.

We pulled back around and Rick's girlfriend got back in the car. She asked where we went. He told her, "We walked around Walmart for a little bit," and that was that. On the way out, though, the young guy Rick was kissing happened to be walking to a friend's house. Rick's girlfriend noticed how flamboyant he was and said, "Wow! That kid has some sugar in his tank." I wanted so badly to tell her that he was not the only one, but I could do nothing but sit and ponder the mess I had gotten myself into.

I have always been an honest person. I have had to later admit every lie I've ever told in my entire life. Lying makes me uncomfortable. Being close friends with Rick's girlfriend and lying to her sickened me for the next few months. It was easier to avoid her. Rick and I were still booked to perform at clubs, so I would drive him around. We'd get fabrics and wigs, which we often stole, and on the way home he would make me pick up his new fifteen-year-old friend and drive them around while they canoodled in the backseat. One day, Rick, the boy, and I went into a McDonalds. They sat on a bench next to each other, and Rick placed his hand in the young boy's pants. This was the final straw. I stepped outside and called my gay father, who lived in Detroit and went by the alias, Noah. I explained the situation and said I could not stand lying anymore. I now forget his advice, but knowing him, I feel it was to tell the truth.

I took one of Rick's cousins (who lived with them) and Rick's girlfriend out to Dunkin' Donuts one day and told them the entire situation. Call me overdramatic, but I felt like I had been trapped under a car and Superman finally decided to show up and lift it off me. Rick's girlfriend was not happy to hear this news, but she shared that she suspected something had went awry. She thought of ways to address him about it, and I realized I would have to face something I hated: confrontation. At that time in my life, I was one of the most non-confrontational people you could have met. People could have belittled me, maligned my name, or stole from my home, and I would have responded to it by blocking them on social media. I hated fighting and arguments; growing up around it was enough for me.

Rick's girlfriend, understandably, did not care. She figured if I had been bold enough to tell her about what was going on, that I should be bold enough to say it again in front of Rick. I was very scared. I had left home and moved in with Rick. Rick was loving and kind to me, and I had betrayed him. When I left home, I was in the mindset that my gay family was all I had. He was acting as my mother, and no one would ever want to be in a situation like this with a parent. I knew if I told the truth that I risked being put out on the street, so I explained this to Rick's girlfriend and she decided to temporarily break up with him.

Rick was upset and knew something was up, but he still had the fifteen-year-old to play around with. I was relieved Rick and his girlfriend had broken up. I couldn't handle the thought of her contracting HIV or anything else from dating a man who slept with other men. It would have broken my heart. But it still bothered me he was dating this high school freshman.

I laugh as I write this. The fact that I wanted the lives of everyone around me to be moral and law abiding while I turned tricks, did porn, and stole amazes me. I think when your life is a mess, you are placed under an illusion that your situation is less detrimental than what it seems. This false reality will have you self-righteously fixing other people's lives, thinking you are above having your own life fixed.

As the weeks went on, I knew Rick trusted me less, but no one was saying anything, so I let a sleeping dog lie. When Friday came, I went to my weekly gig, DJ-ing in drag at a gay bar in the city. I finished the show, and at the end of the night one of the guest performers introduced me to a guy I'll call Dave, and we started dating.

Rick and I, with some other members of our gay family, went to Texas for a week. While we were in Texas, Rick flirted with a few men. I asked him about his "young friend" in front of our other "relatives." I had crossed a line, but he always spoke how he was a man of character, and I couldn't understand why he slept around on this girl and put her at risk for disease. At the end of the trip, someone in the family was obviously troubled over the situation because this individual called Rick's girlfriend and shared the news with her. She was enraged, and I knew as soon as I returned to Chicago everything would hit the fan.

We all walked up to Rick's apartment. She asked "What happened?" in a way that only a black woman can. He lied. She asked again, "Tell me what happened on the trip!" He made up another lie. She then said, "Well, someone said that Kris said…and I need to know what the hell is going on." Rick had asked me in preparation of this event to lie on his behalf, but I couldn't lie anymore. I was tired of lying, so I collected my things and walked out.

Chapter 5

Soul Ties

"Do not be yoked together with unbelievers. For what do righteousness and wickedness have in common? Or what fellowship can light have with darkness?"
[2 Corinthians 6:14]

I was on the street—again. I didn't want to be around my natural family. They didn't understand me and my new life, but the only way to keep my gay family was to lie for the rest of my life. I had to make a tough decision. Rick happened to live above a bar that served dollar drinks every Thursday after a certain time, and to quote Flavor Flav, "You already know what time it is!" I got blackout drunk and went to a friend's house. This was my new life.

While I was in Texas, my new partner, Dave, was also away, so we texted each other daily and became one. Dave was back in town, and I wanted to take him out on a date. We met on the north side and in true Chicago style went to a pizzeria. We were holding hands while walking in the park when he asked if he could tell me a secret. We sat on a bench, and he shared that he had HIV. I didn't know what to think or feel. I had no family (or so I thought), no gay family, and no friends. He wanted to be a part of my life, and I decided that if he liked me and I liked him, his sexual health was irrelevant. We became an item.

Dave was thirty, and I was so focused on his health that I forgot to mention I was nineteen. For months, I led him to believe I was an age that I wasn't. It was not intentional at first, but when I realized I seriously needed to tell him, I grew more and more anxious about it until I couldn't say anything. I signed up for Obamacare and went to a local clinic by my grandmother's house (where I was living at the time) to sign up for PrEP. This is a drug that prevents you from contracting HIV after you have been exposed to it. (**Quick Fact:** A lot of people think they can take this drug and not use protection, but it does not protect you from any other STD or STI except HIV.)

Dave and I formed an unbreakable bond. I later found out this was one of the many soul ties I would have to be delivered from. I started being booked less and less. My drag "career" was basically over and I had no money. Dave paid for everything.

One night, I had gotten drunk at a restaurant with Dave and a few of his coworkers. We had a beautiful time, but I was very uncomfortable because he had paid. I always preferred to pay or at least to offer. I remember going to his house afterward and telling him how bad I felt for letting him foot the bill. He told me it was okay, but for whatever reason, perhaps drunkenness, I broke out in tears. Dave silenced me by being intimate with me. He told me that my crying, or emotional people in general, was a turn on for him. I didn't think anything of that statement until later. It is amazing how we find justification for even the most grotesque of situations.

The seasons changed from fall to winter, and Dave and I began to have problems in our relationship. I eventually found work at a clothing store on Michigan Avenue. He would visit me at work, and although we fought, I was always happy to see him.

Dave introduced me to his friends and invited me to dinners with his family. He eventually found out how old I was, and of course that blew up into an argument, but we made it through. We were committed to one another. Things were on the up and up.

My mother and I reconnected, but she did not take long to get in my ear and tell me things like, "Kris, you know a lot of homosexuals practice witchcraft." "Kris, you know..." I would cut her off. I didn't want to hear what she had to say.

Coincidentally, Dave began to make remarks about wanting to join a church together. I was kind of elated and very relieved. I knew his desire to learn more about God meant that what we were doing was okay. I spent days looking for a church that was "gay friendly." I eventually found one and sent him a web link. I waited for his approval for hours and finally received a text. He wanted to go and was "excited about worshipping together."

Dave, one of his friends, and I started attending the uptown gay church I had discovered. It took me forever to get there on the bus from my house, but I did it for love. I felt like Dave was all I had, so I wanted to rebuild my relationship with God and receive His approval of my relationship.

I stayed the night at Dave's after service one day, and in the morning, I woke up to breakfast. I remember feeling so loved and appreciated. The feeling did not last for long, though, because Dave revealed that he and the pastor of the church we'd been going to for three months had been intimate in the past.

And just like that the same feeling of displacement that originally had made me run to Dave began to radiate from him. I felt small in that moment. I wasn't all that my father wanted me to be, so he left. I was gay, so I didn't feel comfortable around my mom. I wasn't willing to lie for Rick, so I lost my gay family. And now with my lover, I was not loved enough to be given honesty. This is a bad situation. I wanted to be mad, but I had lied about my age to him for months. I had to accept that we were both liars and move on.

Have you ever had a friend in a bad relationship? You constantly watch them get put down by someone they love and will do anything for. It must be difficult. What do you do? I have never had a friend in that situation before, but I have been the friend in the poor relationship. I had a few people I could open up to, and they would give advice, but I never listened.

Lynn Whitfield once said, "The heart wants what it wants and it doesn't care." I stressed a great deal the months following this. My flesh and my spirit were at war. I wanted to stay in my relationship, but I was internally beginning to piece together that every aspect of homosexuality involved some sort of lying or identity crisis. I would always have to be lied to, tell a lie, or live a lie. This cycle is inevitable when you live a life that glorifies the father of all lies, Satan.

My stress developed into anxiety, my anxiety into depression, and my depression into hallucinations. I broke out in hives and boils on every inch of my body, daily for months. I originally thought I was allergic to something because it would even cause me to go into anaphylactic shock.

Dave and I began to fight more and more, and this did not aid my mental health. It was the dead of winter, and winter in Chicago is no joke. I was covered in rashes and blisters, and my partner only spoke to me to argue or have sex.

I told my doctor that I was anxious and depressed all the time, and she gave me a prescription for Citalopram, without even making me speak with a counselor. She said anxiety was a side effect of the preventative HIV meds I was on, and the pills would help. I took the pills for months, and they did not work. I got my dosage increased and began to take Xanax. I drank alcohol with my meds. I figured if my mind was rotting, then my body might as well join in on the festivities.

I walked the streets, scratching and crying. Drag was my comfort zone, so I would sit in my room or at friends' houses, without makeup and wearing wigs. Sometimes, I'd wear leggings, women's underwear, and a wig, or just feminine things. It calmed me down in that state. The other me was starting to become the fulltime me.

One of my favorite films is Sally Field's, *Sybil*. She plays a woman with over twenty different personalities. During this season of my life, I had become this film. My emotions were more than just emotions; each one was a state of being. When I was happy, that was a full-blown happy personality. It had a name, mannerisms, and even a voice. When I got in drag my name was Onyxx, and Onyxx had truly begun to take over. I got to the point where I would walk the streets in leggings, with a bra under my clothes. My time was spent crying, hallucinating, and taking ineffective medication. I had night terrors, where my dreams would either be extremely sexually perverse or would show me sitting in a room filled with fire and screaming.

I began to, in my typical fashion, be angry at God. Most of the adults I knew claimed to be "eagle-eye prophets." When I was younger they would call to talk about what God had revealed to them about me (because God had "assigned me to them"). Or, sometimes, they'd send a text with a vague message. A few years later, here I was, in one of the worst seasons of my life, and no one was sending calls or texts. No one emailed me with a prophetic word or said "come back home." In fact, the only texts I received were from people telling me that leaders were gossiping about me. I guess I had gotten too far gone, or maybe these people never had a good word to begin with. All I can say is that I was mad and wanted nothing to do with God. If I had to suffer and live like this, I would rough it out if that meant I didn't have to go back to church.

Chapter 6

Enough Is Enough

"It is for freedom that Christ has set us free. Stand firm, then, and do not let yourselves be burdened again by a yoke of slavery."
[Galatians 5:1]

One evening, I hopped on the bus to get my prescription refill. Rain was pouring. As I walked into the pharmacy, I heard an elderly man's voice beckon for me. Hurriedly trying to see who called me, I turned around to see no one on the street but distant pedestrians. I sprinted for the pharmacy door to get out of the rain, but I heard the voice call me again. I turned around, and still there was no one behind me. When I put my hand on the door to go inside the pharmacy, an overwhelming urge made me bow on the ground.

Outside on the corner of 103rd and Halsted Street in Chicago, Illinois, God spoke to me clearly and audibly for the first time. He sternly said, "ENOUGH!" I wanted to ask, "Enough of what?" but could not open my mouth. I settled for just thinking a response. God went on to say, "Stop playin.'" He also told me to no longer take those pills.

Outside, getting soaked in rain, the blood of Jesus began the first of many healings in me. The same way that God dwelled over the waters in Genesis, His presence was in that rain. The church my mom attended was up the street. I felt God leading me to walk in there. I sat in the service, cried, tithed the money I was going to use to pay for my prescription, and left.

Not sure what was happening to me, I thought this was a sign to return to church. I started returning more regularly and consumed myself in church events as I had when I was younger. I guess this was a defense mechanism of sorts. Because I didn't have many friends, I drew closer to my cousins and would go to church with them on occasion. I told the pastor about situations in my life. We started meeting regularly, which Dave did not like.

As Christmas of 2016 neared, I scraped together the last of my money to buy Dave a gift. His response was to break up with me. I genuinely wanted to die. My mental health spiraled out of control again, in a far worse way. I cried on the phone to anyone who would listen and eventually exhausted every confidant I had. Sleep had become a distant memory. I was high and black-out drunk every day, trying to wash away a regenerating hurt I did not even know I had. I thought my pain derived from my break-up, but the real reason I was hurting this strenuously was because I realized I had been wasting my life. The peace that was so close and sweet was now bitter and distant.

Repetitively, as a runaway, I heard God tell me to "come back home." At the time, I thought He meant for me to go back to my mother's house or go back to the church. The reality of that statement is that God just wanted me to come back home to Him and be in his will. Eventually, I did that. I experienced what I like to call a "D.I.Y. Salvation," and I call it that because I literally did it myself. It didn't take twenty deacons surrounding me, praying in tongues for me to get saved. God told me to come on home, and I, spiritually, packed up everything I had and returned to Him. I no longer wanted the life of sin or to feel that my life was wasting away. My desires had shifted. It was time for deliverance to start.

This was really when I knew I had to change. I was not going to let myself regress into the muck where I had been before. It was time to be new. I looked up preachers who had come out of situations like mine and found out about Sophia Ruffin and the Comeback Kids. She was a minister in Chicago, who used to be a lesbian. I tuned into her Periscope broadcasts and let them minister to me. I even showed them to my family, who were happy to see me getting into the word of God.

Sophia had a speaking engagement at a church nine minutes away from my house. I needed to go, so my mom drove me. I walked into the church, wearing the world's tightest pants and a floral print blouse (not a shirt, a blouse). On the way there, I was telling God, "Look man, this is it. If it doesn't happen for me tonight, then this is it. I'm tired."

The minister preached a dynamic message about being the real you. It touched me because she exposed something that Satan never wanted me to know, that the real me was not my sexual orientation or my social circle, but the real man was who God said I was in His word.

God says in 1 Peter 2:9 that I am "a chosen generation, a royal priesthood, a holy nation, a peculiar people," and He goes on to say that I should "shew forth praises of the one that has now called me out of darkness and into marvelous light."

Sophia also talked about Psalms 116:6, where the psalmist says, "I was brought low and he saved me."

This was the night! It did not matter what I had been through. She asked, "Does anyone want to become a comeback kid tonight?" I was going to get saved. Remember "Tonight is the Night" by Betty Wright, the song about the girl losing her virginity? She says she's "nervous and trembling." Well, I was nervous and trembling just like her. A six-foot-two nervous wreck fumbled up to that altar and left a changed man. I don't know who placed their hands on me back at the altar, but when I got off the ground it felt as if I had been asleep for twenty years. I wasn't asleep in the prayer line, but it honestly felt as if God had put to rest all the pain I had been through, and He let me experience true peace in Him that night. I got up from the altar and went home, but even though I was able to find rest in God, I still was an unfinished work.

I, somehow, thought that because I had met a prophet and got my life spoken into that I was healed. It was easy for me to let go of all the pain I had faced, but I still hadn't forgiven myself. Because I didn't work on the internal side of things, I started backsliding. Mental disease, anger, and everything else manifested and left my body, but this homosexuality set up camp and would not leave. It took the true love of God to fully pull me out of homosexuality.

One of my favorite deliverance scriptures is 1 Corinthians 15:46: "However that which is not spiritual was NOT first, but that which is natural, and after that which is spiritual." Because of other people's stories, I thought I needed to run and start preaching and evangelizing. I did this, got burnt out, and turned back into my old ways. I even went to a club and hooked up with a guy. The intent was to see if I really was internally changed.

Church people had been telling me that if I was delivered "for real" and sat in the face of temptation, I would not succumb to it. But I did, and when the hookup was over, the guy spoke to me about his day. He said he went to a witchcraft store in Chicago's gayborhood to buy candles for a séance. I maniacally laughed because I thought this was a joke or some sort of scare tactic. He shot me a strange look and asked why I was laughing. When I realized it wasn't a joke, I went up in a fit of rage. I asked him why he shared that with me. He responded by saying, "I don't know. I just thought it was something you would be into."

In that moment, God visited me again, just as He had outside the pharmacy. He said, "Kris, you are so close to me, and yet still so far away. Is this the life you want, because you can have it? Your inner man is messed up. There is no light in you. Witches and warlocks see you as one of them because you refuse to sanctify yourself and enter into the secret place with me. Tonight, I offer you this choice: "If you'll still have me, I'll still have you." I walked out of that club, crying and speaking in tongues. Honestly, I was shook. What my mother had told me was coming to pass in front of my very eyes. She was right. In that moment, I decided that I would never let God down like that again.

As I write, my heart bleeds for homosexuals in the church who think because they're given prophesy regularly means that they are delivered. You have to change internally and turn from your wicked ways. The word of God says in 2 Chronicles 7:14: "Then if my people, who are called by my name, will humble themselves and pray and seek my face and turn from their wicked ways, then I will hear from heaven, and I will forgive their sin and will heal their land."

God cannot change you, for you, without your consent. Every minister in the entire world can lay hands on you, but if you don't make an internal change, God cannot begin the process. When you are being real and serious about deliverance, you don't have to give yourself "tests." You know what's up and so does God.

It has been a very hard journey, but throughout all the church hurt, temptation, mental anguish, indecisiveness, and "etc." I've faced, I continue to live a life of holiness before God. My name is Kristerfur James Reed. I openly renounce homosexuality for holiness. I renounce and openly sever every tie I have with anything unlike the kingdom of God, and I accept the heart, mind, body, soul, and spirit of Christ, allowing them to take complete control over my life. I was able to walk out of the life I lived without any STD or STI. The Lord truly kept and protected, as he promised in His word. That's my story and I'm sticking to it.

I have not come now to condemn anyone. My intent is to show those who feel the way I felt that there is a way out. You can turn your heart back into the father. You can tell Satan to be gone!

Part 2

The Glory:
A Spirit-Led Teaching on
Deliverance

Chapter 7

How to Stay Saved after the Altar (and Things to Avoid)

This section of the book is a breakout deliverance manual. Now that you have heard my story and learned more about my particular struggles, I can give you in-depth details on how I prayed and fasted for my demons to come out. When I first started walking in deliverance, I used to visit churches that had "Deliverance Ministry" in the title. I thought they could help me, only finding out later that I had to help myself. This knowledge I've gained through walking in my own deliverance will be helpful to you and yours. Here are a few pointers:

1.   Deliverance Causes Changing and Shifting.

Change is the act of a person or thing transforming into something new. Shifting is the act of a person or thing moving from one place to another. The difference between the two is that when a change is completed there is no remnant of the previous form visible. A shift, on the other hand, not only leaves a remnant but an option to go back.

An example of shifting:

- Manual car drivers, stick shift, have to shift gears while they are driving. They have the option to move the gear back to the previous place, as freely as they moved it the first time. Yes, of course, the gear shifting occurs according to speed and terrain, but nevertheless, the gears can still be shifted back.

An example of change:

- Every year in the fall, the world experiences a global change. In the spring time, new growth leaps up. Everywhere we venture during the spring season we see beautiful green flora and fauna. The fall eventually comes, though, and nature begins to SHIFT. What was once a bright and friendly green color is now a warm orange, red, or yellowish tone. Ultimately, winter will come and all the leaves will fall and crumble.

- Did you notice that shifting was mentioned when I explained change but that I did not have to use the word change while explaining the shifting process? You cannot have any type of change take place in your life without a shift. You, or something around you, has to relocate before a change can take place. Oftentimes, we shift again, even after the change occurs. Most are generally afraid of this process. No one wants to step out on faith and take a God-inspired move. Stepping out on faith makes you uncomfortable. It takes you out of your comfort zone, but if you don't trust God and his process, then you will never walk in deliverance.

2.   Backsliding is NEVER Okay...but it is normal!

- *"My brethren, count it all joy when ye fall into diverse temptations; knowing this, that the trying of your faith worketh patience. But let patience have her perfect work, that ye may be perfect and entire, wanting nothing." [James 1: 2-4]*

"...he who began a good work in you will carry it on to completion until the day of Christ Jesus." [Philippians 1:6]

There is a common cliché in the church, more so with the older crowd, and it typically is used by those who operate in the "prophetic." I opted to put quotation marks around prophetic because the following phrase is a lie. It goes something like, "Child, God don't care about how you feel? Do you think He cared about how the people in the Bible felt? NO! Now, pick up and do what He has for you to do."

Have you ever seen that happen? I have several times. This is a scare tactic that "prophets," who are giving a word that seemingly is not "sticking," use. They tell a person this to make them realize that the assignment on their life is greater than their feelings and emotions. This is only partially true. Yes, God has tasked us with keeping our hands to the plow and working in His vineyard, but this does not mean that God disregards how we feel, what we think, or who we are. He, very much so, cares about what is going on in our lives.

That is why the word of God says in Psalms 138:8: "The Lord will perfect that which concerns me..."

He cares about you, greatly, and the reason I choose to mention this now is because when I decided to get saved (mentally), "Dave" dumped me. I was so gung-ho about salvation. My mentality, at the time, was if I just left everything behind me I would be better off. The reality was I simply hopped from one extreme to another. I went from being a transgendered prostitute to a walking Jimmy Swaggart revival. I never allowed myself to have that quiet time to process everything. I was unstable on the inside.

Have you ever seen a juicy burger? You loved the idea of it in the commercial or in the picture on the menu, but when you got it and took your first bite, the inside was completely raw. I was the human equivalent of that. I looked edible, outwardly, but my inner man still needed to process. I continued to not let him, though, and that is what led to me backsliding.

3.   Backsliding (cont...) *It's Just a Perfect Illusion!*

Sometimes when you've been married to a sin for so long, severing it causes you to have Phantom Limb Syndrome. When a soldier is shot in war and not able to get immediate treatment, infection sets in. If it was a limb, most likely it would have to be amputated. My *limb* was sin. The Holy Spirit came in, as the infection, and caused the limb to have to be severed. Imagine if one of your arms or legs was no longer there. You would not know what to do. You have had this limb your entire life. You've never had to live without it, but you came in to covenant with Christ and He amputated it.

If you're like me, no matter how long your *limb* has been *cut off,* you will probably still wake up in the middle of the night trying to reach to the right for the glass of water on your nightstand. Then, realizing you no longer have the *limb,* you contemplate flipping over to get it with the other arm or doing without the water all together.

Does that make sense? What I am saying is that sometimes I miss my old sins. Homosexuality, hoeing' (I would've said "fornication," but at the level I was, it's just called hoein'), and everything else I did were done for so long that they became parts of me. There were times a demon would speak to me, and I didn't know if it was me or the demon. That is how in sync I was with what I was doing, but I know the limb has been severed for the better.

Believe it or not, there is nothing wrong with missing sin. It is a normal part of the deliverance process. Allow me to show you what the real problem is. If I can go back to my example for a moment, there are amputees (deliverees) who purchase a fake arm or leg. These false limbs are called prosthetics. These falsies help the amputee cope with the fact that they have a severed limb. If the prosthetic arm is placed correctly in your shirt with some sort of glove at the end or the prosthetic leg is in your Levi's with the correct boot on, you can fool the world into thinking that you are not an amputee.

We have a tendency to think that because the world is fooled by our illusions, that we have fooled God as well. If you believe this, you are sadly mistaken. He sees right through that false leg. There isn't a single illusion that you can pull over on God, and believe me I know a thing or two about illusions. I, a six-foot-two, two-hundred-ten-pound man, used to be a Tina Turner illusionist. I can trick many people, but God saw right through it. Remember that old Nicki Minaj song, "You See Right Through Meeeee"? That is what I sing to God when He calls me out for being fake. Let's keep it real, y'all.

You're probably wondering if the limb amputation was a metaphor for deliverance, then what would buying a prosthetic be considered. The answer is backsliding. See, people buy prosthetics to cope with loss, and we, as deliverees, backslid to cope with not having our sin around anymore. I used get mad at people and have a black and mild. It calmed me down, but how can I say my body is the temple of the living God and defile it without a negative upshot?

Satan tells us to go ahead and sin because it will make us feel good. This is the only time I will ever acknowledge that Satan is right about something. Sin will, in fact, make you feel good. The problem is the aftereffects of sin. He does not show you that when he's trying to tempt you, and this is why the Bible tells us to remain sober and vigilant in 1 Peter 5:8. So many try to make that scripture specifically about alcohol consumption, but the writer was actually saying that we should rid ourselves of *anything* that will take us out of the right frame of mind. The devil is a grand illusionist, very similar to what I used to be, and backsliding does not work unless you are deceived by his trick.

I sat in my room recently doing research on backsliding. This was not some Bible study on those who've backslidden in the word of God, but literally on the word backsliding. Backslide, according to Wikipedia, means "to regress; to trip backwards or revert to a previous, worse state."

Being the avid scholar that I am, I was compelled to research the words used in the definition. One phrase really stuck out: "trip backwards." Normally, when one trips it is over something causing them to fall forward. Generally, when a person falls backward it is because they have been pushed down by another person. This made me think. In order to "trip backward," you would've already been walking backward.

Is your mind blown? Mine was. What this means is that you don't just up and backslide. If temptation is avidly finding you on the regular, there is a possibility you are welcoming it. Some of us plan to backslide; I am guilty of this. I won't go to church for a few weeks. I won't pray. I won't fast. This is to prepare my body for sin. If I'm not full of prayer and time with God, then committing a sin will be easy, right? I know you don't want to admit it, but you probably also have things you do before you intentionally sin. This cycle needs to be broken immediately.

There are two ways I will go about breaking it. The first is teaching because Hosea 4:6 says we suffer only because of a lack of teaching. The second is through prayer.

The more I studied on what it truly meant to backslide or "trip backwards," God revealed things to me. I looked up synonyms for the word "trip," and to my surprise, the first word I saw was "fall." The reason I was surprised was a trip normally leads to falling, but they are not the same thing. They are a cause and an effect, yet they were viewed as synonyms. Do you know that one of the devices of the enemy is to confuse us about his strategies? If we know what he is doing, we can foil his attempt in doing it. Whoever made "trip" and "fall" synonyms on thesaurus.com was sadly mistaken. Tripping means to stumble. Falling means you stumbled and fell.

I was a clumsy child. As I shared previously, I acted a lot in grammar school, and one year we put on a production of Schoolhouse Rock Jr. I was a member of the chorus in this scene, and I tripped over my robe and fell on stage, in front of the entire school and parents. Everyone laughed. For the rest of that year, I was the butt of every joke I heard in passing.

That was a time I tripped and fell, but there were other times I tripped and was able to recover before I fell. This is what separates these two words. Spiritually speaking, when you stumble God throws a lifesaver in the water for you, even when the stumble is intentional. Imagine you are newly celibate and free from masturbation and pornography, as well. You open your Instagram app to see a naked person on your timeline. You have a lifeline here. See, on Instagram there are three periods in the upper right hand corner of every photo. When you touch them an option that says "see fewer posts like this" will become available to you, and you can rid yourself of those sorts of photos.

I used that example, because I used to blame what others posted on social media as an excuse to behave sinfully all the time. Most of us are going to hit that button. Carnal people, such as us (me, you, and a dog named Boo), go on the page and skim through for other explicit photos. We may get ballsy enough to follow these pages and like the posts. We have the lifeline to get out of sinful waters but will most likely still choose to drown. This is what the devil wants.

The Bible says in James 1: 2-4 (KJV): "My brethren, count it all joy when ye fall into diverse temptations; knowing this, that the trying of your faith worketh patience. But let patience have her perfect work, that ye may be perfect and entire, wanting nothing." This scripture is one of my favorites and coincides with another one we all know, Philippians 1:6. The NIV says it like this: "...he who began a good work in you will carry it on to completion until the day of Christ Jesus."

That was rather loaded, I know. Let's break it down. James 1 (KJV) says, "The trying of your faith worketh patience." The NIV, on the other hand, says, "The testing of your faith produces perseverance." This translation felt the need to use the word "testing." Generally, when you take a test, unless you are someone like me who takes the Facebook personality quizzes to find out "What Kind of Church Goer You Are?", you can only pass or fail.

The Latin root of the word "fail" is *fallire*. *Fallire* means "to *trip*, cause to fall." Isn't it just plain wild that "backslide" is defined as meaning "to trip backwards" and "fail" means "to trip"? The end result of backsliding is an inevitable failure. You will not see this is in the moment, but it will happen.

All my analyticals, who are deep and wonderful, may be pondering how I know this is the work of Satan. I'm glad you asked. *Fallire*, further explained by dictionary.com, means "to deceive, trick, dupe, cheat, or elude." The last time I checked, someone was mentioned in the Bible for stealing, killing, and destroying. His name is Satan. Have you ever brought a product from a mall kiosk? The seller made the item look great, but when you got home your new $40 teeth whitening system was defective.

Don't allow Satan to make your new life defective! Tell Satan to "be gone." When you repetitively backslide, a cycle is formed. You don't go to church on Sunday to be cleansed from sin Monday to Saturday only to return the following Sunday for another cleansing. Hosea 4:6 says children suffer only because of a lack of knowledge, so take this *teaching* and end your cycle!

4.   When All Else Fails, Trust the Process

You're not going to be "fully delivered" overnight. It may actually take years for you to walk in complete holiness. A friend once told me, "You have to eat an elephant one bite at a time" #TrustTheProcess. I know this comes off intimidating, but I have to keep it real with you. I didn't commit myself to God and stop liking men just like that. I had to accept the mind of Christ, pray, and fast regularly. I woke every day at 5 a.m. to go into my basement and speak in tongues. I did this to gird up my spirit man for things I would face during the day.

We live in a world that is anti-holiness and pro-lust. You cannot go on Instagram or Facebook without seeing #EggplantFriday posts of men in grey sweatpants or the new thing called #TheBeardGroup, where women rate posted pictures of men in the comments. Social media, in my personal opinion, is a demonic trap set up to draw ex-homosexuals back into the lifestyle. I know that may sound crazy to you, but if you were on my side of this book, you'd understand. When I was fresh out of the lifestyle, I would delete all my accounts on social media, but then I would miss them and recreate them the following day. The level of extra is unfathomable. I eventually was able to gain self-control. The reason I share this is because I want you to know that despite what anyone has to say, you have to do what is best for you. Others, especially your friends who are still in it, will not (not may not, but **will not**) understand your deliverance, but hey, this is about you! Deliverance is the only place in Christianity where God wants you to be selfish. You have to get yours before you can help anyone else.

Also, FYI, let me forewarn you. You—sir or ma'am—are about to get HURT IN THE CHURCH. Yes, the "Church Hurt" (whatever that is) is about to be serious. People will question your deliverance. People will not understand how they've had a gay relative their whole life who is no longer gay (or whatever sin you have come out of). You will be asked all types of crazy questions.

Quick story: When I first walked out of homosexuality, I went to bishops and deacons and other leaders asking them to be my spiritual father. None of them would associate with me because of my past. They didn't want me to make them look like they were gay. This was not only incredibly offensive, but it's the exact opposite of what Christ would have done. There is even a female pastor I grew up around whose entire ministry was based around deliverance from homosexuality. I scheduled meeting after meeting with her, and she rescheduled me every time until I got the hint. Yet, whenever I go on Facebook, she's talking about how God sent her to do deliverance in the LGBT community. The old me would be petty and comment on the posts, but the new me knows that #ChurchHurtIsNotReal. Yep, I said it. Church hurt is not real, and here's why: Romans 8:11.

The spirit of God is in us! How can you say the church hurt you, when you are the church? In the olden days, according to the Old Testament, God's presence was stored in the church. Only the priests could enter, and we (the normal folk) had to wait outside in the outer court to hear from God. But now, the veil has been torn, and the presence of God is available to all men.

We are the church, you guys. Accept that. If someone in a building (called a church) hurts you, guess what? That's just a rude person. That isn't church hurt; it's just "hurt" hurt. Some of these people in church are not the real deal. They speak in tongues and prophecy and will turn around after service and gossip with the same mouth. You have to know God for yourself.

God commanded us to fellowship with our brethren. He told Noah to gather **two** animals of each kind for the ark. Jesus sent the apostles out **two** by **two** in Mark 6:7. We have to work as a team. We have to be together. When you are offended by a coworker, you don't stop going to your job, so don't deprive God of your worship by not going to church. Take everything negative that happens to you in a church with a grain of salt, and know that the test cometh for the working out of your perseverance. When these things happen to you, it's not because church is judgmental and evil. That is a lie the enemy wants you to believe. The real reason we face trials in the church is because the church is God's way of perfecting his soldiers.

Matthew 5:39 says, "If anyone slaps you on the right cheek, turn to them the other cheek also." The Bible says in Isaiah 54:17 that no weapon formed against us will prosper. Since we know the weapons formed against us will ultimately fail, the ones that do prosper have to get permission from God to do so. I know you think I'm lying because God would never do anything to hurt you, right? Wrong! God uses adversity to humble us. Trust the process.

Chapter 8

Deliverance On-The-Go: Prayers That'll Keep YOU

Because of the spirits I've faced, I thought it was fitting to insert some DIY deliverance prayers into *Satan, Be Gone.* These prayers are to help you, the reader, unlock and break off any bondage you may be in. I encourage you to read the prayers aloud, even if you don't believe they apply to you. You will be surprised by what may arise in you as you read. You may feel angry at certain sections and sad at others.

Sometimes, you may put down this book and feel like you can't read it anymore or even throw it across the room. That is because what is in you does not want you to get free. These feelings are spirits in you that hold a resonance with what was in me. You have to fight it and stay concentrated.

We pray out loud to let the devil know we want no part in whatever he has placed in us and to let God know we are ready and thirsty for it to be cleaned out. Take a few moments to bring old memories to the forefront. This may seem counterintuitive, but I promise it is a part of the process. I encourage sitting in a quiet room, with soft worship music playing. Bask in the presence of the Lord before entering this prayer, and make sure that you are ready for your bottled up feelings to be dealt with.

Morning Prayer

Father God, in the name of Jesus, I thank you for waking
me up and starting me on my way.
God, I ask you to help me throughout this entire day.
Keep my mind in check.
Keep my heart in check.
Keep my loins in check.
Keep my mouth in check.
Help me to remember that I am a kingdom ambassador,
and that every word I speak reflects the kingdom.
Help me to remember that I am your child.
I give you full permission to convict me at the very
moment I do anything that misrepresents the kingdom.
Don't let me lead people away from you, but allow me to
live a prosperous life that would make non-believers draw
nigh and learn more about you.
Thank you, God, for giving me another day and another
chance to live for you.
I will not let you down.
In Jesus' name,
Amen.

"Before Bed" Prayer

God, I call this bed, this pillow, this room, and this entire
house to be blessed.
I will have sweet sleep, in the name of Jesus.
Incubus will not visit me in my dreams tonight.
Succubus will not visit me in my dreams tonight.
I cancel the assignment of every ungodly soul tie that wants
to remind me of itself in my slumber.
None of those sprits or soul ties are welcome in my house.
I sanctify and dedicate this house to you, God, right now in
the name of Jesus.
I plead the blood right now, over every stronghold,
principality, or spirit of wickedness in a high place.
I will not wake up horny in the morning, but I will wake up
holy.
It is so you in son Jesus' name,
Amen.

"Before Work or Church" Prayer

God, I offer myself up to you right now.
I am getting ready to be around other people.
God, I ask you to deal with me and my emotions right now.
Do not let me be easily offended.
Let me operate in supernatural maturity.
Allow me to operate in supernatural patience.
Let me see the good in people today, Lord.
Help me to not respond to ignorance by being ignorant
myself.
God, let me evangelize (on my job/at church) today.
Help me to win souls for you.
Purge me with hyssop right now, so that I won't judge
others by their outward appearance, and miss an
opportunity to win souls and advance your kingdom.
I call the manifestation of this prayer to come forth now, in
the name of Jesus.
Amen.

"When You're Horny and Want to Backslide" Prayer

God, listen...I am operating in the flesh.
I have been thinking about sex all day.
God, please keep me near the cross.
Help me to desire less of man and more of you.
Help me to lust after and long for the advancement of your kingdom, and nothing else.
Purify me right now, oh God.
Mortify my members.
Purge me that I may be white as snow.
God, you said in your word that the Holy Ghost was a comforter.
I need him to come comfort me right now.
Holy Ghost, help me to not text me exes or look at porn.
And, if I do slip up and text them, allow them to be turned off by me and not respond.
Make me be so holy that they feel uncomfortable entertaining my "You Up?" texts.
It is so.
Amen.

"Homosexual Residue to Fall Off (Men)" Prayer

God, you said in your word that you are a potter and that I
am your clay.
I pray that you will make and mold me in the man that you
called me to be.
Mold me, oh God.
I want to walk like you.
I want to talk like you.
I want to carry myself like you God!
I no longer want to "switch" when I walk.
I no longer want my voice to be high.
Allow me to represent you.
Allow me to act just like you and your son Jesus.
Mold me into a perfect husband, that I may find a wife and
start a family.
Mold me into a perfect son, that I may bring honor unto
my biological parent, and unto the men of God whom
you've placed in my life to mentor me.
God, change my body.
Allow me to be built for your glory.
Change my taste in clothes.
God, take the taste and desire to perform certain sex acts
out of my mouth.
Take the will to do things unlike you out of me.
Let me be holy and righteous before you.
It is so.
Amen.

"Homosexual Residue to Fall Off (Women)" Prayer

God, here I am, your daughter.
Help me, God.
I no longer desire to carry myself like this.
I only want to carry myself like you.
Help me to be a Proverbs 31 woman.
A woman that is called blessed.
Give me my femininity back.
Grow me.
Mold me into the perfect wife, that I may be the apple of
my husband's eye.
Mold me into the perfect daughter, so that I may gloriously
represent my mother and the women of God whom you've
sent to mentor me.
Change my taste in clothes.
God, take the taste and desire to perform certain sex acts
out of my mouth.
Take the will to do things unlike you out of me.
Let me be holy and righteous before you.
It is so.
Amen.

"Deliverance from Masturbation" Prayer

God, help me to be disciplined.
Help me to stop touching and rubbing on myself.
Turn my hands into instruments of praise, that bring you
glory and please you and not me.
Give me will-power.
Teach me how to rest in you.
Teach me how to lean on when I feel weak.
Replace the fire of lust that is sitting in my chest with the
refining fire of the Holy Ghost.
I cut off every stronghold in the name of Jesus.
I cut off every "spirit-husband," "spirit wife," fantasy
woman or man that I have masturbated thinking about.
These soul ties will no longer hold me down.
I command them to loose me and let me go in the name of
Jesus.
I am free in Christ.
I will fast without temptation.
I will live a normal everyday life without having to take
mid-day breaks to do this secret sin.
I am free in Jesus name right.
I seal this prayer right now, by asking God to build a hedge
of thorns and fire around me that Satan cannot penetrate.
And, I commend the devil to get thee behind me right now.
Satan, Be Gone!
It is so, and in Jesus name,
Amen.

"Staying Delivered" Prayer

God, help me to keep my promise to you, and not go back.
God, Help me to understand why I can't go back.
Help me to understand that others are watching me.
Help me to understand that I am someone's hope.
Help me to understand I cannot let you down anymore.
Give me a righteous circle of friends.
Give me godly mentors, who want the best for me.
Place me in a church where I can grow and blossom.
Place me in a church where I can reach my full potential.
Allow me to be the change that I want to see in the world.
Allow me to change the world and not let the world change me.
Anoint me with oil, spiritually, right now.
Anoint me for my destiny.
Anoint me for my assignment.
Anoint me to go back and snatch others out of the gates of hell.
Help me to stay on the right track.
In Jesus' name,
Amen.

Conclusion

Greater Works than These
Shall Ye Do: Prophecy

Son/Daughter, understand that you are now, what is called, a Comeback Kid. A comeback kid is someone who was in darkness but came out of it and is going back to snatch others out. Because of your deliverance, God has blown the fires of evangelism on you and your life. You will never be the same. You can never be the same. You won't ever be the same.

You will not fit in anywhere you go. You will always stand out. In the beginning stages of this, you will be angry at God. Understand that this is only happening, because God himself is spotlighting you. You are a chosen generation. You are a royal priesthood. You are a child of the most-high God. Do not get mad at God. He's just showing off. You've gone through the fire, and you've come out gold. Let God flex on His gold.

The spirit of "I'm not good enough" has officially been broken off of your life. I obliterate, annihilate, destroy, implode, and cut it at the root in the name of Jesus Christ of Nazareth. You will not think that you are not worthy of God's love because of your past. For those with a past are the very people Christ came back for. You have been made clean, right now, through the prophetic word. John 15:3 says, "Now ye are clean through the word which I have spoken unto you."

And the spirit of God says that you shall cast out demons by the legion. You shall perform great exploits and works for the glory of the word. Miracles, Signs, and Wonders will follow you as long as you believe, for it says so in the word of God. You will walk alone for a season, but then just like Elijah, God will send you a successor.

Just like Esther, you will have to speak out boldly in uncomfortable situations, even if it means death. Just like the prostitute in 1 Kings 3, you will have to decide to give up something you love just to see it and yourself both grow. Finally, just like Jeremiah, there will be an unquenchable fire shut up in your bones.

You have welcomed all of these trials into your life by deciding to walk upright before God. It will pay off. Hold fast to the promises of God, which the word says are "ye and amen." You are a king's kid. You are who God says you are. Because you are a king's kid, you will not hold your head down. You will not be discouraged. You will not feel small. You will not be anxious. You will not walk in despair. For the glory of the Lord is upon you.

In the same way that Jesus released the disciples in John 14 and told them they would perform greater works than He, Rapper and scribe Taylur Holland famously exclaimed, "You were delivered to be a deliverer. Today, I, a man of God, release you now unto the world to set the captives you've been assigned to free. You have the power and authority to change the world. Go forth. It is your season."

About Kristerfur Reed

Kris Reed is a dynamic man of God with a story like no other. After years of life as a homosexual and transgender woman in Chicago, IL, he decided to exit a life of sin and enter a chaste walk with the Lord. Kris spends his free time ministering and praying for people bound in situations unlike God. He has truly been delivered to be a deliverer. He believes in John 3:17, "The son of God was sent into the world, not to condemn it, but that the world by him might be saved." Through sharing the message of the cross, in an open and loving manner, he has been able to win souls and greatly impact the kingdom of God, at the young age of twenty.